Introduction

These materials are designed to accompany the book *Ma'at's Feather* by Juliet Desailly. (Published by The Book Guild Ltd, Pavilion View, 19 New Road, Brighton BN1 1UF. ISBN 978 1 84624 273 1).

The book tells the story of Qen, a boy who lives in ancient Egypt and is designed for Key Stage 2 children. These materials provide creative, cross-curricular lesson ideas based on the story, many of which would fit comfortably into the Literacy Hour and others of which support teaching and learning in the foundation subjects.

The Creative Curriculum

One of the difficulties of trying to provide children with a more creative curriculum is in finding texts which are appropriate to Literacy teaching but offer opportunities for exploring wider curriculum links. *Ma'at's Feather* was specifically written with this in mind. Each lesson idea has parallel learning objectives in two or more subject areas and uses creative, enquiry-based approaches such as role play, hypothesis, debate and research. Lessons include a strong emphasis on paired or group work and build skills in social and emotional learning.

The materials

Whilst providing ideas for exciting, engaging lessons the materials are designed to be used flexibly by teachers as best fits their class and situation.

As a children's novel *Ma'at's Feather* is written to appeal to an audience aged 7 – 11 years old. In a school context this covers a wide range of ability and so some children may need more support with the text than others. The school year and term in which ancient Egypt is studied also varies from school to school so the cross-curricular lesson ideas themselves may need to be adapted for age or ability.

The lessons, howev
appeal to children at their own level and are generally differentiated by outcome. Many are based on enquiry and many also involve speaking and listening or drama activities.

A range of lesson ideas are included, based on each chapter of the book (and some ongoing activities). It is not supposed that all the activities suggested will necessarily be used. Teachers should select those that seem most appropriate to their class.

Key Questions

At the beginning of the materials for each chapter there are some 'Key Questions'. Some of these are explored in the lesson ideas, others may be the stimulus for class or group discussion or reading journal activities.

Context for Learning

Above all, it is hoped that the book, in conjunction with the lesson ideas will provide a rich context for learning. The children will have the chance to build empathy with a boy whose life is very different from theirs but who has to deal with problems and issues that are timeless. They will discover fascinating information about a civilisation that never fails to engage children and have the chance to explore similarities and differences in customs, lifestyles, morality, hopes, dreams, fears and dilemmas across the millennia.

Ma'at's Feather

Synopsis

Qen is a young boy living with his father and older brother in ancient Egypt. The family farm land for the temple. When the Nile floods the men work as labourers helping to construct a new temple building. Qen is small for his age and longs to be tall enough to help work with the men.

Qen gets his wish and joins the men working at the quarry. He works as a water boy and enjoys mixing with the other men. As the flood waters begin to recede there is an accident and his father is fatally injured by a falling stone slab. After his father's death and funeral Qen and his brother realise they may lose their home and livelihood if the temple decide they cannot continue to farm the land.

The temple officials are persuaded to let Qen and his brother prove themselves and they begin the back-breaking work of ploughing and sowing the land. However, Qen's brother begins to act strangely and is often missing from the fields; he even leaves the house after Qen is asleep. Realising this Qen follows him one night and discovers he is meeting with some men that Qen does not know. It sounds as if they are plotting something.

Qen asks his brother what is going on but his brother refuses to tell him, hinting only that he has big plans for a better future and that Qen should relax and trust him. Finally Qen's brother takes him to meet Khon, one of his mysterious friends. Khon tells Qen that they plan to rob the tomb of a rich man who died recently. Qen is small enough to get through the hole left unmortared when the entrance was bricked up. A few small portable items would be enough for them to sell and start a new life in another town.

Qen is horrified, he believes that interfering with the dead will doom him in this life and the next but Qen's brother and Khon use a mixture of persuasion and moral blackmail to try and influence him. Qen is left to make his decision, knowing that if he does not cooperate then his brother will leave without him and he will be left alone.

Qen joins the others at the tomb and climbs through the hole and down into the burial chamber. He is amazed and terrified by what he sees. He brings some items to his fellow tomb-robbers but they send him back for more. When he finally returns it is to find that they have been discovered and the others have fled.

Qen is arrested and questioned. He does not disclose the others' part in the robbery in the hope that they at least will get away and start a new life. He is taken down river to be tried. At his trial he is found guilty and sentenced to be left in the Western Desert. He expects to die there… but in the distance he sees approaching riders, strangers from a neighbouring country who stop for him…

Ma'at is the goddess of order and justice. Her feather is used to weigh people's hearts after death to see if they were good or bad in life. Qen finds a feather as he has to make his most difficult decision, it becomes a symbol for him of the right and wrong of what he does.

Prologue

Key Questions

Why is there a prologue? What does it do? What do we find out about the central character in the prologue? Where and when is the story set? How do we know? What kind of place is the story set in?

1. Literacy/Geography

Learning Objectives

Literacy
To deduce and infer information from a fiction text
To retrieve and combine information from non fiction texts.

Geography
To identify and describe what places are like.

Activities:

- Read the prologue and discuss what information we are given about the place the main character is in. Where could it be?

- Look on a physical map of the world or globe and identify where deserts are found. Is there any pattern to the part of the world they are in? (Hemisphere? Poles? Equator?)

- Link this information with other deductions from the text (this could also include the blurb and cover) to make an informed decision as to where the story is set. Identify the position of Egypt on a map of the world and a map of Africa. Look at a map of Egypt; identify the River Nile and where the desert is.

- Use non-fiction books or the internet to begin to research the geography of Egypt – climate, types of landscape, crops grown etc. Alternatively use good quality photographs to ask and answer the question 'What is this place like?'

Ongoing Activities

1. Literacy/Geography

Learning Objectives

Literacy
To retrieve, select and describe information and ideas.

To organise ideas into a coherent structure including layout, sections and paragraphs.

Geography
To identify and describe what places are like.
To recognise how people's lives are influenced by the climate and natural resources where they live (this is a more challenging concept and may suit older or more able children or require some support and modelling).

Activities:

- In each chapter we are given more information about life in ancient Egypt and how life there is influenced by the climate and natural resources. Collect this information on post-it notes as each chapter is read. At a suitable point (the end of Chapter 5?) review all the post-it notes and collate the gathered information. This might form part of a Literacy lesson on organising non-chronological writing into paragraphs or with subheadings.

2. Literacy/Geography

Learning Objectives

Literacy
To retrieve, select and describe information.

Geography
To represent a place as a map.

Activities:

* In each chapter we are given information about the countryside where Qen lives, nearby places and their relationships to each other. Ask the children to work in pairs or small groups to make a map of the area. This should include: Qen's house, fields, river, town (with temple), quarry, two cemeteries, the Western Desert. Explore how features are represented on maps (e.g. symbols, keys).

* Ask the children to look at each other's maps. Where there are differences, discuss: do we have any information from the text that would clarify where things are? Are there any geographical clues? (e.g. would they build the town where the river flooded? Will the fields be near the river?) Stress that there is no absolute right answer but we can make sound judgements based on evidence.

* Continue to mark on the map where incidents in the story take place and routes that characters take.

3. Literacy/History

Learning Objectives

Literacy
To learn what a glossary is and how to use one.

History
To learn about features of a period.

Activities:

* Look at the glossary in the book. Discuss how it is arranged and what its purpose is. How is it different from a dictionary? Or an encyclopaedia? How can we use it?

* As unknown words or concepts are discovered in the text encourage the children to use the glossary. Discuss whether the glossary gives enough information on each subject. What can we do if we want to know more?

* Children could add to the glossary as they read. They could investigate and research some entries further and extend them to become entries for a children's encyclopaedia of ancient Egypt with illustrations and additional text.

Chapter 1

What do we find out about the central character in this chapter? What do we find out about life in ancient Egypt? Who else lives with Qen? What do we find out about them? Where does Qen live? Who does the land belong to? What does his family do?

1. Literacy/History

Learning Objectives

Literacy
To retrieve, select and describe information and ideas.

History
To make deductions from primary and secondary source material.

Activities:

- Discuss what we discover about Qen's life in this chapter. Where does he live? What does he do? What other people are involved? What do his family eat and drink? Etc.

- Ask the children to construct a family tree for Qen with the names and relationships of his family.

- Give the children access to good quality colour pictures of scenes from rural life in ancient Egypt from wall paintings and shabti figures. Ask the children what we can find out about life in ancient Egypt from the pictures.

- Ask the children to draw a picture of where Qen lives with him and his family in the picture. They will need to research what his house, clothes etc would look like if they are not already sure from previous research.

Chapter 2

Key Questions

What work is Qen doing at the beginning of this chapter? What is he trying to prove by working so hard? What do we discover about Qen as a friend? How is your life similar to Qen's and how is it different?

1. Literacy/PSHCE

Learning Objectives

Literacy
To understand story structure.

PSHCE
To recognise and name feelings.

Activities:

- Qen has many different feelings during this chapter and moves between different places. Discuss these. Can the children make still pictures of the different feelings?

- Ask the children to divide the story up into different sections and draw a diagram or 'cartoon' representation of each section as a storyboard. Label each section briefly with what Qen is feeling and what is happening in that section.

- Ask the children to compare their storyboards with a partner. Discuss whether everyone broke the episode into the same number of sections. What were the differences? Are they significant?

- This chapter is like a mini-story – it has a beginning, middle and end. Ask the children what they think the climax of this chapter/story is. Could there be more than one climax? If so, where are they?

2. History/Geography

Learning Objectives

History/Geography
To make deductions from primary and secondary source material.

To use evidence to investigate what a place is like in the present and the past.

To say what has changed and what has stayed the same.

Activities:

- Qen goes to the River Nile in this chapter. Look at pictures or video clips of the River Nile at the present time. Ask the children 'What is it like? What is it used for today?'

- Look at pictures of activities on and around the Nile in ancient Egypt. What was it like then?

- Compare the activities on or around the Nile in ancient Egypt and today. What has changed and what has stayed the same?

- Link back to Qen's life. What are the similarities and differences between his life as a child in ancient Egypt, and that of a child in the UK today?

SEAL Links
The above activities for this chapter could be used to make links to building skills in empathy, self awareness and managing feelings.
Including:

- Making choices about behaviour and predicting consequences

- Belonging to a group, being a friend

- Understanding the feelings of others

Chapter 3

Key Questions

Is Qen a good brother? What evidence is there? How does it feel if you get lost or lose someone else? What do you think the festival is for? Why do we have festivals? What do they achieve for individuals and the community? There is the first hint of a mystery in this chapter, did you notice it?

Can you find examples of imagery in the writing? What does it achieve? Why do people ask for help in their prayers?

1. Geography

Learning Objectives

Geography
To understand how rivers may flood and how this may be useful or damaging.

Activities:

- Show the children video clips of rivers flooding including positive and negative images.

- Explain/explore how a river may at times have more water in it than usual e.g. from snow melting or heavy rain. Point out that the place where it floods may be far from where the extra water enters.

- Discuss how the flooding was helpful to the ancient Egyptians. Why is it not always helpful for a river to flood?

- If relevant look at any local places where there is a risk of flooding. What is being done to reduce risk? There may be websites, local newspaper reports etc to use for further research.

2. PSHCE/SEAL/Literacy

Learning Objectives

PSHCE/SEAL
To understand how it feels to get lost or to lose someone.

Literacy

To understand how imagery can enhance description.

Activities:

- Look at the text of the part of the chapter where Qen loses his sister and ask the children to identify passages where he describes his feelings by relating them to something else (using similes).

- What do the similes do to help us understand Qen's feelings? Notice that his feelings relate to his stomach, how else might we experience feelings of shock, fear, anxiety?

- Ask the children to work in pairs to describe occasions where they have been lost or lost someone else. What did they feel? Share some of these.

- Ask the children to come up with their own similes to describe their feelings.

- At the end of the chapter Qen finds his sister, what might his feelings have been then? Why does he cry then and not earlier? What simile might best describe his feelings of happiness and relief?

3a. History/ICT

Learning Objectives

History
To discover what gods the ancient Egyptians believed in.

ICT
To use the internet for research.

Activities:

- Explain that people in ancient Egypt believed in many gods, some were special to different places or were thought to help in particular situations.

- Ask the children to research the roles and appearance of the gods in ancient Egypt on a suitable website (eg www.ancientegypt.co.uk/gods).

3b. PSHCE/SEAL/RE/DT

Learning Objectives

PSHCE/SEAL
To recognise anxiety or worries and how we can relieve these feelings.

RE
To explore the part of prayer that asks for help.

DT
To investigate stable structures.

Activities:

- The townspeople write prayers to the god and give them to him by placing them by his statue. How do people today pray? Share the children's own experiences. (This could link with work on RE QCA **Unit 6A**: Worship and community - Generic **Section 2**: How do adherents of different religions talk to god?)

- Discuss how when we have worries, sharing them can help (Link to SEAL theme 'Good to be me').

The Horus Stela

- As DT QCA unit 3D (Photograph frames) use Section 1, the investigative, disassembly and evaluative activities to explore methods of making things stable.

- Look at a good picture of the Horus stela, on many websites or in the Chapter *Magic and Medicine* in the *Eyewitness Guide Ancient Egypt*. Why might Horus have been holding scorpions, snakes, lions etc? Elicit that they were dangers and sources of worry to ancient Egyptian people.

- Ask the children what worries them in life in the 21st century. Ask them to discuss with a partner what they would want to ask for protection from in a modern stela. Who would they ask for protection from? Would it be from God or from society?

- Ask the children to design their own stela with images and/or writing to show what they are asking for protection from (and from whom, if appropriate). They should then use one of the techniques they have investigated to make their stela stand upright (using the usual design – plan – make – evaluate cycle).

4. Music

Learning Objectives

Music
To identify the features of dance music.

To compose music for a purpose.

Activities:

- Play the children passages of dance music from different periods and cultures. Ask them what the music makes them feel like? How would they move to this music? (Explore this physically if possible).

- Ask the children to identify the features that make music suitable to dance to (e.g. rhythm, regular structure, pace).

- In Chapter 3 there is dancing in a procession. Discuss when this happens today (e.g. carnival) Possibly look at video clips of dancing in a procession.

- Explore the type of instruments the ancient Egyptians might have played in a procession (e.g. clappers, shakers, bells) Ask the children in groups to use similar percussion instruments to compose a piece of music to dance to in a procession.

- Use the music to form their own processional dance.

SEAL Links
The above activities for this chapter could be used to make links to building skills in empathy, managing feelings and social skills.

Including:

- Understanding the feelings of others
- Managing feelings of worry
- Caring for other people

Chapter 4

Key Questions

Why does Qen enjoy his time working so much? How do we react when we are teased? What new information do we learn about life in ancient Egypt? How did the ancient Egyptians organise themselves?

1. PSHCE/SEAL/Drama

Learning Objectives

PSHCE/SEAL
To understand that not everyone feels the same about different situations.

To know how to tell if your behaviour is upsetting someone.

Drama
To create roles and dialogue to explore issues.

Activities:

- At the beginning of the chapter Qen is teased and called 'Strongman' by the men in his team. He doesn't mind. Discuss why he doesn't mind and why someone else might have done.

- Discuss teasing and nicknames. Can the children come up with some criteria for acceptable and unacceptable teasing. You might use a chart or provide pairs with a writing frame in two columns e.g.

We think teasing and nicknames are OK when…

We think teasing and nicknames are wrong when…

- Divide the children into groups. Ask them to prepare and act out two scenes where teasing or using nicknames are a) acceptable and welcomed and b) unacceptable and unwelcome. Show and share the scenes and discuss what they have discovered.

- Ask the children how they can tell if their own behaviour is welcome or upsetting to someone else. What might they a) see or hear in the other person b) do themselves to find out?

2. History/Thinking skills

Learning Objectives

History
To use secondary sources for research.

To understand features of a period (ancient Egyptian building and social organisation.)

Thinking skills
To reason and hypothesise.

To devise structures for organisation.

To use de Bono's six thinking hats to aid problem solving.

Activities:

- Ask the children what they can find out about building in ancient Egypt from books or the internet. They should differentiate between large-scale building projects (pyramids, temples) and domestic building. (This could be an activity for a single group while other groups research other subjects and then they can report back to each other).

- Ask the children to imagine they are the chief temple officials. They need to organise many different projects: building a new temple, producing food for the community year on year, organising a festival. Divide them into teams (committees) with one of these challenges for each team. What do they need to consider to get the jobs done? What structures will they need (administrative, organisational)? How will they organise a workforce? How will they acquire and distribute resources?

- Draw together what the children have discovered about the scale of social organisation in ancient Egypt.

- Analyse how they had to think about the task to organise their project; possibly refer to de Bono's six thinking hats and consider whether they used all six in their deliberations. (With prior knowledge of the thinking hats, they could, of course, each be given one to use in their meeting).

3. PSHCE/SEAL/Speaking and Listening

Learning Objectives

PSHCE/SEAL
To understand what motivation and perseverance are and how we can achieve them. (Links to SEAL theme 'Going for Goals').

Speaking and Listening
To offer reasons and evidence for their views, to listen to another speaker and respond to another person's opinion appropriately.

Activities:

- Ask the children to name some chores at home or school, jobs they do that they really don't like. List them on the board. Then name some that they don't mind or quite enjoy.

- What is the difference between the jobs you enjoy and the ones you don't? Is it just the nature of the job or who you do it with or how you approach it?

(This little story might help.
"When I was a little girl we had a wooden floor that needed polishing. We would rub the polish on then put on old socks, play some music and 'skate' on the floor until it was shiny. It was such fun that all my friends wanted to come round and join in when we polished the floor.")

- You might want to watch the video clip from the film 'Mary Poppins' where she sings 'A spoonful of sugar' and discuss "You find the fun and snap, the job's a game".

- Ask the children to work in groups to choose one or more of the jobs they don't enjoy and discuss how they could make it more fun. Each group should report back to the whole class.

- Relate this back to Chapter 4. Why does Qen enjoy working in the quarry even though it is such hard work?

Also see SEAL materials in 'Going for Goals' on setting targets and breaking jobs down into stages.

The above activities for this chapter could be used to make links to building skills in empathy, self awareness, managing feelings, social skills and motivation.

Including:

- Making choices about behaviour and predicting consequences

- Belonging to a group

- Understanding the feelings of others

- Knowing yourself and standing up for yourself

- Persistence and target setting

Chapter 5

Key Questions

In this chapter and the one before what new information do we learn about Qen, his father and his brother and the sort of people they are? How might people react to receiving very bad news? What do we know about doctors in ancient Egypt?

1. PSHCE/SEAL/Literacy

Learning Objectives

PSHCE/SEAL
To understand feelings of shock (and loss and grief).

Literacy
To use descriptive language.

Activities:

(This is a sensitive issue. Care should be taken if children have experienced loss or bereavement. See also SEAL materials for the theme 'Relationships').

- How did Qen feel when he got the news of his father's accident, when he saw his father and when his father died? What words are used in the text?

- Talk about feelings of shock when something unexpected happens e.g. when you hear bad news or hurt yourself or are very scared. How can it affect you physically?

- Ask the children to think about a time they had a shock – it might be quite a small thing. Ask them to generate descriptive phrases to describe how they felt. They might link this to work on similes.

2. History

Learning Objectives

To use secondary sources for research.

To understand features of a period (ancient Egyptian medicine).

Activities:

- Ask the children what they thought about the doctor in this chapter. What drugs did he use? Why did he not do much to the wounds? Why was he 'intoning a strange phrase over and over'?

- Ask the children what they can find out about medicine in ancient Egypt from books or the internet. (This could be an activity for a single group while other groups research other subjects and then they can report back to each other).

SEAL Links

The above activities for this chapter could be used to make links to building skills in empathy and managing feelings.

Including:

- Understanding my feelings
- Understanding the feelings of others

Chapter 6

Key Questions

How does Qen feel at the funeral and the next day? Why do we have funerals? What new things does Qen learn about his brother? What physical signs are there that Amen is under stress?

1. History/Literacy

Learning objectives

History
To understand features of a period (funeral and burial customs).

Literacy
To deduce and infer information from a fiction text.

To retrieve and combine information from non fiction texts.

Activities:

- Explain to the children that rich and poor people in ancient Egypt had very different funerals and burials. Qen's father was a poor man.

- Ask the children to discover from the text of Chapter 6 what happened at Qen's father's funeral.

- Ask the children to use non-fiction texts to research burial and funeral practices for rich and poor people.

- Children could communicate their findings in a poster or labelled pictures.

2. PSHCE/SEAL

Learning objectives

To know how remembering good things about people we have loved who are no longer with us can help us deal with our loss.

(This is a sensitive issue. Care should be taken if children have experienced loss or bereavement. See also SEAL materials for the theme 'Relationships').

Activities:

- In Chapter 6 people start to remember and tell about good memories of Qen's father. What do they remember?

- Discuss how it's good to remember things when you don't see a person any more. Not just if they've died but if they or you have moved away.

- Ask the children to think about a person they miss (there might be a child who has left the class if they can't think of someone). Can they think of some good things to remember about that person?

- The children can record their memories in individual, personal ways. They might write them on paper leaves and stick them on a twig to make a memory tree or make a mini-book with decorated pages with the memories in.

- The children should be able to keep their memories private if they wish but can share them with a friend or an adult if they want to.

3. Literacy

Learning objectives

To construct a persuasive argument.

Activities:

- At the end of Chapter 6 Amen has to persuade the temple official that he and Qen should be able to stay on their farm. What arguments does Amen use?

- Give the children some topics they have to persuade someone about (not moving house, being allowed out with a friend your parents disapprove of, being given more pocket money etc.) Ask them to work in pairs to discuss and decide what persuasive points they could use.

- Put two pairs together, each pair in turn should try and persuade the others (in an appropriate role)

- 'Spotlight' some pairs to share their arguments and comment on their effectiveness.

- The arguments could later be written as dialogue or in the form of a letter if appropriate.

SEAL Links
The above activities for this chapter could be used to make links to building skills in empathy, managing feelings and motivation.

Including:

- Understanding my feelings

- Understanding the feelings of others

- Planning to reach a goal

Chapter 7

Key Questions

Why do you think Amen is behaving as he does? How do you think Qen is feeling? How did they farm in ancient Egypt?

1. History

Learning Objectives

To discover what farming was like in ancient Egypt.

Activities:

- Ask the children to discuss what information they have from the book so far about farming techniques and life for the farm workers. Draw out the information and list.

- Give the children access to pictures from tomb paintings of farming and photographs of relevant shabtis. What else can they discover about farms in ancient Egypt? (NB Qen's family were quite poor farm workers, other farms were much richer).

- Ask the children to draw a picture entitled 'Farming in ancient Egypt' to illustrate as many features as possible. This could be done in groups.

2. Literacy/PSHCE/SEAL

Learning Objectives

Literacy

To deduce and infer information from a fiction text.

To be able to write notes.

PSHCE/SEAL

To understand and name feelings.

Activities:

- Remind or introduce children to the features of notes and process of note taking.

- In Chapter 7 Qen and Amen are not getting on well. Ask the children to look back over previous chapters and make notes on what their relationship has been like. (This will also include the skills of skimming and scanning which might need introduction).

- Discuss how both Qen and Amen might have been feeling at the time in Chapter 7. Write a list of those possible feelings. Ask the children if they have ever felt any of those feelings and in what circumstances.

- There are several references in the book to Amen not wanting to marry. The children might discuss possible reasons for this. Reasons given might include sexual orientation and, if appropriate, might give an opportunity to discuss this.

SEAL Links

The above activities for this chapter could be used to make links to building skills in empathy, social skills and managing feelings.

Including:

- Understanding my feelings
- Understanding the feelings of others
- Seeing things from another point of view
- Making choices and solving problems

Chapter 8

Key Questions

Who is Amen meeting and what are they planning? Why is Amen dissatisfied with his life? What is Qen feeling?

1. Literacy

To deduce and infer information from a fiction text.

Activities:

- Amen is behaving in a mysterious way in this chapter. Discuss what could be going on and why the children think that.

- Ask the children to hypothesise about what they think Amen is doing and go back over the text so far to find evidence about Amen that might prove their point. This could be done in groups.

- Ask the children to present their point of view about what Amen is doing and share the evidence they feel supports this.

2. PSHCE/SEAL

To understand and name feelings.

Activities:

- Qen is feeling very confused. Ask the children to generate feelings words to describe his state of mind at different points in the chapter. They should then draw/write them in a whirlwind around him.

SEAL Links

The above activities for this chapter could be used to make links to building skills in empathy and managing feelings.

Including:

- Understanding my feelings
- Understanding the feelings of others

Chapter 9

Key Questions

Qen has a difficult decision to make – what thoughts are going through his mind? What is he feeling? What advice would you give him? Why is the feather important to Qen? When did we hear about the feather before? What do we find out about death and the afterlife in ancient Egypt?

How does Qen reach his decision? What choices do you think he had? Do you think he made the right decision?

1. Literacy / PSHCE

Learning Objectives

Literacy
To empathise with characters and debate moral dilemmas portrayed in texts.

PSHCE
To consider social and moral dilemmas.

To talk and write about their opinions and explain their views.

Activities:

- Read Chapter 9 and discuss: Khon and Amen are trying to persuade Qen to help them. What arguments do they use? What are Qen's responses?

- Form a 'Conscience Alley'. Choose a child to be Qen. The rest of the class make two lines facing each other. One line will give reasons Qen should help Khon and Amen, the other line will give reasons why he should not. Ask the child playing Qen to walk slowly down the 'alley' listening to the advice he is given. Choose other children to get a chance to be Qen.

- Ask the children who played Qen which reasons they took notice of most and why.

- Ask the children to write a letter of advice to Qen as an agony aunt, giving their reasons why he should or should not help Khon and Amen.

2. Literacy / PSHCE

Learning Objectives

Literacy
To make deductions about a character and his motives from the text.

To present ideas clearly and effectively.

PSHCE
To consider social and moral dilemmas.

To talk and write about their opinions and explain their views.

Activities:

- Ask the children to discuss with a partner or in a small group why they think Qen made the decision he did and whether they think he was right or wrong. They should try to use evidence from elsewhere in the story to show what might have contributed to his decision.

- Ask the children to write their responses to the two questions using the format: I think… because. (You might want to use a writing frame for this).

3. History / Literacy

Learning Objectives

History
To understand ideas and beliefs of people in the past.

Literacy
To gain information from a text.

Activities:

- Ask the children to work in small groups with a copy of the text of chapter 9 to find out all they can about the following topics:
  - Death and the Afterlife
  - The goddess Ma'at
  - Attitudes to status and people's place in society (this is more challenging and might be given to older / more able pupils).

- After sharing what they have learned from Chapter 9 they could use non-fiction texts to research the topics (and issues of burial practices) further, making notes or writing up their findings as appropriate.

SEAL Links
The above activities for this chapter could be used to make links to building skills in empathy and managing feelings.

Including:

- Making choices about behaviour and predicting consequences

- Belonging to a group

- Understanding the feelings of others

Chapter 10

Key Questions

What different feelings does Qen have during this chapter? How are they described? How does the feather make him feel? What is the tomb like? What do we find out about everyday objects and the life of the rich and poor in ancient Egypt? What do we find out about their attitudes to death?

1. History

Learning Objectives

To research what objects wealthy ancient Egyptians put in their tombs and what that tells us about their lives.

Activities:

- Ask the children what objects Qen found in Khnumhotep's tomb.

- A great deal of our knowledge about ancient Egypt comes from objects archaeologists have found in tombs. Ask the children to look at pictures of some of these (using books or the British Museum website) and to choose three they really like. What do these three objects tell us about the person who owned them or about life in ancient Egypt?

2. PSHCE/SEAL

Learning Objectives

To understand feelings of fear.

Activities:

- In this chapter Qen feels really frightened. How is this described?

- Use an 'emotional barometer' * (a circle with five divisions) and write 'I am feeling frightened' in the centre.

- Ask the children to work in groups to think of five words to express the gradations of fear from being just a little afraid to being the most afraid you could be.

- Ask the children to write these five words in sequence in the divisions around their 'emotional barometer'. The children should then decide where, on their barometer Qen would have been in this chapter.

- Children could then describe times they have been frightened and use the 'emotional barometer' to show what level of fear they felt. Or they could hypothesise about different possible experiences and rate them on their 'fear barometer'.

*For more information on emotional barometers see the DFES's SEAL materials.

SEAL Links
The above activities for this chapter could be used to make links to building skills in empathy and managing feelings.

Including:

- Understanding my feelings

- Understanding the feelings of others

- Managing feelings of fear

Chapter 11

Key Questions

Qen is asked a lot of questions – he doesn't answer all of them truthfully. Why is that? What do his decisions show us about the type of person he is? What advice would you have given him if you were there? Why?

1. PSHCE/SEAL/Drama

Learning Objectives

PSHCE/SEAL
To explore feelings of guilt and responsibility.

Drama
To present events and characters through dialogue.

To use drama strategies to explore stories and issues.

Activities:

- Qen decides not to tell on his brother and his friends. Discuss what his reasons were. Do you think he was right or wrong and why?

- Divide the children into groups to act out a short situation where someone is caught doing something wrong but others involved don't get caught. At the end of the scene the character who was caught is asked who else was involved.

  (Some suggestions for situations are:

  You are caught bullying someone

  You are caught stealing

  You are caught cheating

  You are caught playing inside when you should be in the playground

  You are caught playing 'chicken' on the railway tracks

  You are caught smoking

  You are caught passing notes to someone when you should be working)

- Share the scenes and discuss them.

- Put the character who was caught with two (or more) 'conscience advisors'. They give him or her advice as to why he or she should or should not tell with reasons.

- What should each character do? And why? Discuss the possible outcomes.

- Can the children make any generalised 'rules' as to situations in which you should definitely tell someone about others who were involved?

SEAL Links
The above activities for this chapter could be used to make links to building skills in empathy, self awareness and managing feelings.

Including:

- Understanding my feelings

- Understanding the feelings of others

Chapter 12

Key Questions

What happens on the journey down the Nile?
What is the court like? What different feelings
does Qen have? How are they described?
What do you think of the judgement?

1. PSHCE/SEAL/Literacy

Learning Objectives

PSHCE/SEAL

To understand cause and effect and taking
responsibility.

Literacy
To deduce and infer information from a fiction text.

Activities:

- On the boat Qen goes over all the events
wondering why things had happened and what
would have happened if… Ask the children to
draw a picture of Qen's face in the centre of a
piece of paper and write all of the questions
that Qen might have been asking himself in
thought bubbles around him. (This could be
ready prepared for the children if required).

- Ask the children to work with a partner to
answer Qen's questions.

2a. PSHCE/SEAL/Literacy

Learning Objectives

PSHCE/SEAL

To feel empathy for a character.

Literacy
To write persuasively.

Activities:

- Remind or introduce the children to the
features of a persuasive text.

- In ancient Egypt people did not have lawyers in
court to speak for them, they spoke for
themselves. Ask the children whether they think

Qen explained himself well enough in court. What
would they have said if they were Qen?

- Ask the children to imagine that they are Qen.
They should write a speech to persuade the
judge that they should be set free.

2b. PSHCE/SEAL

Learning Objectives

To decide what is fair and unfair.

To understand why there are rules and laws and
how they are enforced.

To consider different methods of justice.

Activities:

- Ask the children to imagine that they are the
judge at Qen's trial. They should work with a
partner to discuss what judgement they would
have come to and what actions or punishment
they would have given Qen and why.

- Share and discuss their opinions. What would
have happened if someone the same age had
committed the same crime nowadays?

SEAL Links
The above activities for this chapter could be used
to make links to building skills in empathy, self
awareness and managing feelings.

Including:

- Understanding my feelings

- Understanding the feelings of others

- Making choices

Epilogue

Key Questions

How does the epilogue link with the prologue?
Is there a change in how Qen feels between the prologue and the epilogue?
What is the significance of the title of the book?

What do you think happens at the end? What do you think happens after this story is over?

1. Literacy/PSHCE

Learning Objectives

Literacy

To empathise with characters and infer characters' feelings and consequences in logical explanations.

To identify and comment on the structure of a text.

PSHCE
To consider taking control and responsibility for actions.

Activities:

- In Chapter 12 Qen said he felt like a playing piece in a game, now he decides to walk west and then run towards the approaching strangers. Ask the children to discuss the significance of these actions. For children needing more support you might list these and some other of Qen's actions (going to meet Amen, going into the tomb, refusing to give his name etc) and ask the children to discuss and decide whether Qen is taking responsibility for and control of his actions in each case or not.

- The story ends on a 'cliff hanger'. Ask the children to discuss why they think this is, do they like these kind of endings? What do they think happens next?

- The children could plan a sequel to Ma'at's Feather.

About the author

Juliet Desailly is a long-time resident of south London, and her background is in primary education and writing educational material. Although she started out teaching drama, English and music in secondary schools and has also been involved in theatre companies, since the mid-1980s she has mainly taught in primary schools and has also run training courses and worked in an advisory capacity within the field of education. From 2001 to 2004, she was deputy head of a Sydenham primary school, and since then she has been a freelance educational consultant specialising in cross-curricular links and planning for a creative curriculum and is a member of the Department of Early Childhood and Primary Education at the Institute of Education.

She has written a large amount of educational material, including teachers' notes for a television music programme, two series of Infant History for BBC Radio, and materials for the current DCSF's 'Social and Emotional Aspects of Learning' (SEAL) resource. She also contributed sample lessons and a videoed lesson for the Excellence and Enjoyment materials on integrating key aspects of learning and social and emotional aspects of learning into the curriculum.

Ma'at's Feather is her first children's novel.